मंगल मूरति मारुत नन्दन सकल अमंगल मूल निकंदन

FLOW
of
GRACE

मंगल मूरति मारुत नन्दन सकल अमंगल मूल निकंदन

मंगल मूरति मारुत नन्दन सकल अमंगल मूल निकंदन

CHANTING THE *HANUMAN CHALISA*

FLOW *of* GRACE

ENTERING INTO THE PRESENCE OF
THE POWERFUL, COMPASSIONATE
BEING KNOWN AS HANUMAN

KRISHNA DAS

मंगल मूरति मारुत नन्दन सकल अमंगल मूल निकंदन

All blessings come from the Grace of the Guru.

I offer this recording to my guru,
Sri Neem Karoli Baba.

To Sri Siddhi Ma and to the ongoing presence
of Sri Jivanti Ma.

To the elder devotees of my guru who showed
the way to devotion.

To Dada and my Indian parents,
Mr. and Mrs. KC Tewari.

To all the Saints and Great Beings, known and unknown,
who have shed their light on the Path.

For Janaki, my daughter.

For my mother and father.

For "AH."

For all the people who come and sing
with me, I thank you all from the
bottom of my heart.

May all beings be Happy!

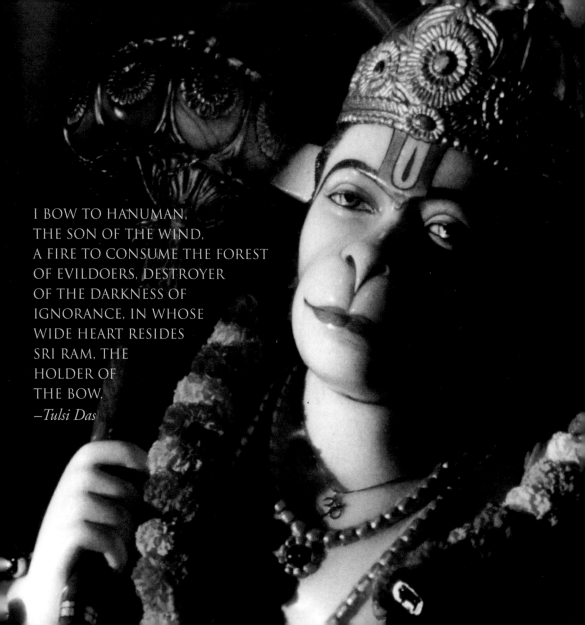

I BOW TO HANUMAN,
THE SON OF THE WIND,
A FIRE TO CONSUME THE FOREST
OF EVILDOERS, DESTROYER
OF THE DARKNESS OF
IGNORANCE, IN WHOSE
WIDE HEART RESIDES
SRI RAM, THE
HOLDER OF
THE BOW.
—Tulsi Das

CONTENTS

INTRODUCTION

I went to India in the fall of 1970 to meet Neem Karoli Baba (Maharaj-ji), after having heard about him from Ram Dass. Ram Dass had recently returned to the United States in 1968 after meeting Maharaj-ji and spending about a year in India. I had heard about Ram Dass from some friends, and together we went to see him at his father's home in New Hampshire where he was staying. As soon as I walked into his room, I intuitively knew that whatever it was I had been seeking was real. I didn't know if I would find it, but I knew it existed in the world. Although I didn't realize it at the time, that moment changed my life. As I spent more time with Ram Dass, I realized that it was Maharaj-ji's presence I was feeling, and a year and a half later, I went to India to meet him.

By the spring of 1971, I, along with some other Westerners, had gone up to the Kumaon Hills, the magical foothills of the Himalayas, where Maharaj-ji was staying at his Hanuman temple in Kainchi. We were staying at the Evelyn Hotel in the nearby hill station of Nainital. The hotel was owned by the Sahs, a family of Maharaj-ji's devotees. Nainital was built around an ancient crater lake and was a sacred place for the Goddess. We felt like we were in heaven.

SRI
NEEM
KAROLI
BABA

Every day—or as often as Maharaj-ji would allow—we would make the one-hour trip by bus along the narrow winding roads through the mountains to see him and spend the day at the temple. Each time we arrived, we were fed a huge, delicious meal of *puris* and potatoes and given a little booklet with a picture of Hanuman on it. I had a pile of those booklets—all written in Hindi—in my room at the hotel. One day, I happened to ask someone at the temple about them and was told that they contained a prayer to Hanuman called the *Hanuman Chalisa*. The *Hanuman Chalisa* is a hymn of forty verses that describes and praises the life, character, and exploits of Hanuman. At that moment, I had the idea to try to learn it so we could sing it to Maharaj-ji.

Rameshwar Das, another American, and I began to learn the Hindi alphabet. We transcribed the whole prayer and were taught a melody by an Indian friend. It took the whole rainy season and summer to begin to feel comfortable singing the *Chalisa*. By the time we returned to Nainital and Kainchi, most of the other Westerners had copied it into their books and had begun to learn it as well. We hadn't even memorized six verses when one afternoon we were called to the front of the temple where Maharaj-ji was sitting. He was very excited and said, "Sing the *Chalisa!*" We were completely unprepared but managed to sing the few verses we knew. He laughed and was very happy.

We quickly became an official part of the "show." When Indian devotees came to see him, Maharaj-ji would often call us and have us sing the *Chalisa*. No matter how many times we did it, he would always look totally surprised—as if it were the first time he had ever heard it. With a look of joy and amazement on his face, he would laughingly tease his Indian devotees for their lack of devotion and sincerity, saying, "Look at these people. Out of their love for God, they have left everything behind in America, while you wicked, greedy people come to see me out of your own selfish desires!" Of course, it was all part of his unique way of teaching everyone their own special lesson.

We began to chant the *Hanuman Chalisa* as a way of bringing ourselves into Maharaj-ji's physical presence. It was a way of expressing our love and devotion to him. For us, Hanuman and Maharaj-ji were the same. Chanting the *Chalisa* to Maharaj-ji helped us enter into the love that his presence embodied. It became a way of deepening our relationship with him, and ultimately with ourselves.

It has been thirty-three years since Maharaj-ji left his body, and chanting the *Chalisa* has become an even more powerful way for me to enter into the flow of Love and Grace. In the *Chalisa*, we bow to the great beauty, strength, and devotion that Hanuman embodies; we also begin to bow to that place in ourselves. The *Chalisa* inspires us to try to become like him, to make the mirror of our heart as clean as Hanuman's so that we can become aware of the great beauty and love that lives within us, our own true nature, the One without a second. This is the Great Being known by many names throughout the many spiritual and religious traditions in the world.

Photo & illustration credits:
Cover and table of contents photos © Parvati Markus
Pages ii, iv, viii, 6, 22, 31, background images © Shutterstock.com
Page 2, 37, 38, 66 photos of Maharaj-ji © Balaram Das
Page 6 © Rameshwar Das
Page 24 painting "Red Monkey" © Cindy Wilborn 2006
Page 32 © www.alamy.com
Page 44 © Jaya Prasada
Page 47 © Nina Rao
Page 57 photo © Keshav Hunter
Page 69 by HWT (Australia) Bill McAuley
A good faith effort was made to discover the copyright holder of each image included. If you have any information about uncredited images, please contact the Sounds True Art Department at (303) 665-3151.

By His Grace: A Devotee's Story, Stories about Neem Karoli Baba, by Dada Mukerjee, Hanuman Foundation Publishing, © Hanuman Foundation, 1990.

Every effort has been made to contact the license holders for quoted content in this book. Any questions about permissions should be directed to the permissions department at Sounds True: 413 S. Arthur Ave., Louisville, CO 80027.

The NewHINDI SANSKRIT and TransINDIC fonts used in this book are available from www.linguistsoftware.com.

For a free catalog of wisdom teachings for the inner life, call (800) 333-9185 or visit www.soundstrue.com.

THE STORY OF HANUMAN

 Before we begin to talk about Hanuman, it is important for me to mention that I do not see this story primarily as "Hindu mythology," or as a story that has no relevance outside of Hinduism. The beings referred to as the "Hindu gods" are the way that one of the oldest cultures on Earth experiences the One Reality that shines brightly in many forms. Each culture and each religion has its own colored glasses through which it sees the universe. The reports from the frontlines differ only in form, not in substance. They are all looking at the same thing. Maharaj-ji would continually remind us that it is all One. Over and over he said, "Hanuman, Christ, and Krishna are the same," and "all paths lead to the same goal." Again and again, he turned us to the oneness of life, reminding us that "the same blood runs through everyone's veins."

Hanuman in the Hindu Tradition

We meet Hanuman in the great Indian epic, the *Ramayana*. My favorite versions of the story are *The Song of Rama: Visions of the Ramayana* (Devi Vanamali, Blue Dove Press, 2001), *Ramayana* (William Buck, University of California Press, 2000), and *Sri Ramacharitamanasa* (Goswami Tulsi Das, Gita Press, 1991).

Tulsi Das, masterful Hindi poet of the sixteenth century, is also the author of the *Hanuman Chalisa.* He was a great poet-saint who created a huge body of devotional songs and prayers, mostly to Ram and Hanuman. His *Ramacharitamanasa* (The Lake of the Story of Ram) is a "folk" version of Rishi Valmiki's original *Ramayana.* Every chapter is a deeper descent into the heart of devotion.

THINE OWN CONSCIOUSNESS, SHINING, VOID, AND INSEPARABLE FROM THE GREAT BODY OF RADIANCE, HATH NO BIRTH NOR DEATH, AND IS THE IMMUTABLE LIGHT.

—*Buddha Amitabha, quoted by Sri Krishna Prem*[1]

The basic story is that of the battle between good and evil. It takes place on many levels. There was a demon king named Ravana who had conquered all the Earth and the gods. He was very powerful and the incarnation of evil. In order to destroy Ravana and reestablish Dharma on Earth, God incarnated as a man. He was named Ram and was born as the son of the king of Ayodhya.

The story begins with the gods *(devas)* finding out that Ram, the Supreme Being, is going to incarnate. To help him with his mission, the gods decide to take birth on Earth.

From *Bhakraj Hanuman:*

> *Suddenly speaking "Ram Ram," Lord Shiva broke his samadhi. Parvati Devi saw that Lord Shiva, moved with an extraordinary sentiment, was looking her way. Standing before him with joined hands, she humbly spoke, "Lord! At this time, how may I serve you? Is there something you wish to say? It appears from the movement of your face that this is so." Lord Shiva said, "Beloved! Today a greatly auspicious resolve has risen in my heart. I am thinking of he who I continuously meditate upon, whose name, by constantly repeating, I live in never-ending delight, whose true form I remember and become absorbed in ecstasy; he who is my God, my Lord, is taking birth and coming into the world. All the gods want to take birth with him for this opportunity to serve him. Then shall I remain deprived of this? I also will go there, and, by serving him, the aspiration I have cherished throughout the ages will be fulfilled. My life will be fruitful."[2]*

Shiva transmitted his essence through Pawan, the Wind-God, and Anjani, a beautiful Vanara woman, to incarnate as Hanuman. (The Vanaras are believed to have been a race of man-monkeys.) Ram and his three brothers were born in Ayodhya and the play on Earth began. Over the course of time, Ram was married to Sita, his eternal consort and the incarnation of the goddess Lakshmi, who was born as the daughter of King Janaka.

Due to a debt that Ram's father owed, he was forced to banish Ram from the kingdom for fourteen years on the eve of Ram's coronation. Happy to do whatever his father asked, Ram, Sita, and Ram's brother, Lakshman, left immediately for the forest. This was all part of the Divine Plan. While they were staying in the forest, Sita was kidnapped by Ravana and taken to Lanka, his island kingdom. In great despair, Ram and Lakshman wandered all over the forest, looking for Sita.

Meanwhile, Hanuman, Shiva's emanation, grew up and became the adviser and friend of Sugriva, the king of the Vanaras. It was in the service of Sugriva that Hanuman approached Ram and Lakshman in the forest and introduced himself to them. After meeting Ram, Sugriva pledged the help of all the monkeys (the gods incarnate) to look for Sita. When the monkeys were about to leave on their search, Ram revealed part of his true nature by giving his ring to Hanuman with a message to deliver to Sita, knowing that Hanuman would be the one who would find her.

All the Earth had been searched except for Ravana's kingdom in Lanka, which was eight hundred miles across the ocean. Hanuman was quietly sitting by the ocean while the other monkeys were trying to decide how to get across. None of them were able to jump over and get back. Jambavan, the king of the bears, saw Hanuman sitting there and said: "O son of the Wind-God, you are as strong as your father and a storehouse of intelligence, discretion, and spiritual wisdom. What undertaking in this world is too difficult for you to accomplish, dear child?" When Hanuman heard this, he jumped up and said, "I'll do it. I'll jump over the ocean and find Mother Sita."

He jumped across the ocean and found Sita there. After relieving her despair by giving her Ram's message, he jumped back across the ocean and reported to Ram where Sita was being held prisoner.

Sacinandana Swami says that Hanuman is "an example of discovering our forgotten potency. Up to the point where he crossed the ocean with one big leap, he was not aware that he had this potency, but because he wanted to do seva, this potency came out, empowered him, and proved that the word "impossible" is a word not existing in a devotee's dictionary.

This quality of unlimited inner strength can only be awakened when it is in the service of Love. God is love, and when we align ourselves with that love and act in the service of that love, anything is possible.

The monkeys went on to accomplish the impossible, building a bridge across the ocean by which Ram and his army crossed over to Lanka to fight Ravana's demons. After many other miraculous exploits by Hanuman, the demons were defeated and Ram killed Ravana, liberating Sita.

That is the basic storyline, as written by Valmiki in the *Ramayana*. Tulsi Das retells the story in a devotional way to inspire people with the love of Ram. Reading his *Ramacharitamanasa* rewired my heart. It is actually a transmission of love itself. It opened up a new capacity for love and devotion in me. Tulsi Das describes Ram's beauty and the love flowing from his eyes, the way he moves, and the rapture everyone feels as they gaze on him. As the characters in the story are transported into the realm of love, we are also lifted into that embrace. Many times Hanuman will watch as Ram meets and blesses people, and he too will get lost in ecstasy, seeing the compassion and beauty of the Lord. As we read these scenes, we are also touched and transformed by them.

Tulsi Das also describes the extraordinary devotion of Hanuman. After Sita and Ram were reunited, Sita offered her pearl necklace to Hanuman. It was very valuable, as Ram had given it to her. She wanted to honor Hanuman by giving it to him. Hanuman looked at it and, one by one, began to bite and crack each pearl and then throw them away. Sita was shocked and asked Hanuman why he was destroying the necklace. She thought he was acting like

राप

a foolish monkey. Hanuman explained that as far as he was concerned, something could only be valuable if the Name of Ram was inside it, and so he was looking to find the Name. Not finding it, he threw the beads away. Sita asked him what value he had, since Ram's Name was not inside him. Hanuman then tore his chest open with his nails and everyone saw that inside him, inscribed on every bone, muscle, and organ, was the Name of Ram.

At one point, Ram and Lakshman are captured by Ravana's brother, Ahiravana, who takes them to a hell world, where he plans to offer them

सकल अमंगल मूल निकृंदन

as a sacrifice to the Goddess. They
are surrounded by serpents and
demons. Lakshman, who was
forever respectful of his brother,
stayed quiet but could not stand
the fact that they were doing
nothing about getting out. Finally,
he could not control himself any
longer and asked Ram, "You are the
Lord of the Universe. Why are you
not getting us out of here?" Ram replied,
"When the universe is in trouble, they come to me,
but when I am in trouble, I wait for Hanuman!"

It was through reading the *Ramacharitamanasa* and chanting the
Hanuman Chalisa that I began to understand the subtlety and power of
the path of devotion and the sublime way that love can transform the
hardest heart into the heart of a saint. It is love that brings meaning to
our lives. The path of love goes right through the middle of every heart.
No one is locked out. No one is turned away. No one is unworthy. The
love that lives within each and every being is Bhagavan; it is Ram, Buddha
Nature, the Atman, the Great Goddess, the Self, the One. It is who we
are—our own True Nature, radiant and shining like a million suns.

The dance of devotion is so beautiful. We long to be with the Beloved, to feel that presence of love in our hearts, but in the eyes of God, we have never been separate—not even for a second.

Tulsi Das wrote:

> I speak to Hanuman
>> Thus do I speak to King Ram,
>> the perfect, gentle one . . .
> I speak to Shiva Himself, the ocean of grace.
> Be aware! And listen all!
> Of joy and sorrow, love and anger, of virtue and vice,
>> the creator made all.
> Of time and nature and fate,
>> Ram is the doer.
> So I have known this Truth,
>> having dwelt upon it in my heart.
> Ah Lord, only quench this moping and grieving.
> What is there that You can't do?
> Let me grow silent
>> having known
>> that I reap what I have sown.

There is also a beautiful *bhajan*, or devotional song, written by Tulsi Das,
in which Ram explains to his brother Bharat (who remained behind during
Ram's exile in the forest) who Hanuman is. He says:

> *Oh Brother Bharat, I can never repay the debt I owe to this monkey.*
> *My whole story would have been lost in this world if it wasn't*
>   *for Hanuman.*
> *He jumped eight hundred miles over the ocean, found Sita, saved*
>   *Lakshman's life, killed the demons, and not once did pride arise*
>   *in his mind.*

Tulsi Das continues:

> *I am recounting the greatness of Hanuman in the very words that came out*
>   *of the Lord's mouth. Oh Brother Bharat, I can never repay the debt I*
>   *owe to this monkey.*

In the Valmiki *Ramayana*, Ram asks Hanuman, "What is your relationship with Me?" Hanuman answers, "As a body, I am your servant; as an individual soul, I am a part of You and You are the whole; as the Self, we both are one. This is my firm conviction." Hanuman lives in the One without a second, at one with the universe. He never loses this awareness, but in order to help Ram complete His work—which is to destroy spiritual darkness and restore Dharma—he remains identified with being the servant of Ram, all the while knowing that Ram is the real doer, accomplishing all his own work.

सकल अमंगल मूल निकंदन

Hanuman in the Tibetan Tradition

Hanuman is present not only in Hinduism but in other spiritual traditions as well. Robert Thurman quotes His Holiness the Dalai Lama as saying that the Tibetan people are descended from a celibate monkey god. A demoness fell in love with the monkey god and threatened to kill herself unless he mated with her. The monkey asked Avalokiteshvara if he could break his vows of chastity for one night in order to save the life of the demoness. He was given the green light, and the Tibetan people are descended from that mating.

Hanuman is also mentioned in Tibetan Buddhism's *Kalachakra Tantra*. The Kalachakra, or Wheel of Time, is an allegory for the passage of time in the universe. It tells the story of Shambhala, an enlightened kingdom ruled by the benevolent king Raudra Chakri. Raudra Chakri is identical with the Kalki Avatar—the final incarnation of Vishnu mentioned in Hinduism— and with Maitreya Buddha, the future Buddha.

As the story goes, the rest of the world has descended into a dark age, but the Buddhadharma is guarded by the warriors of Shambhala. In time, a war breaks out between the forces of good and evil, and the lands south of Shambhala are taken over by a barbarian named Krinmati. Having conquered these territories, Krinmati sets his sights on Shambhala.

Knowing that the kingdom is about to be attacked, Raudra Chakri calls together his army under the command of his generals, Hanuman and Rudra. The army is vast and mighty and has the assistance of the twelve great gods as well. With so much strength, Krinmati's army does not stand a chance. Hanuman and Rudra emerge victorious and set the stage for the final showdown—for the avatar to complete his mission, destroy the great demon, and reestablish Dharma on Earth. Hanuman's role serving the avatar in the *Kalachakra Tantra* is the same as in the *Ramayana,* which takes place in an earlier age.

Hanuman in the Chinese Tradition

In the Chinese Buddhist tradition, there is a fable called "Monkey." An old monk named Tripitaka travels to India to receive the Dharma teachings and bring them back to China. On the way, he meets a rascally monkey with great powers. Through the strength of his purity, the monk converts the monkey into a guardian and protector of the Dharma. With the monkey's help, Tripitaka is able to overcome all obstacles and bring the Dharma to China.

WHY CHANT THE
HANUMAN CHALISA?

In 1996, I visited Maharaj-ji's temple at Kainchi. At the time, one of his very old great devotees, Shri Kehar Singh, was also staying there. I spent many hours talking and sitting with "Poppa," as he was called. As I was getting ready to leave for America, he gave me his blessings and a bit of advice. He asked me if I knew why we sing the *Chalisa*. I said, "To praise Hanuman." He asked me if I thought that Hanuman needed me to praise him. "Of course not," I said.

Then he explained, "Even as a child, Hanuman had such strength and was so mischievous that he would cause havoc all around. One day, his playfulness was disturbing a saint during his worship. The saint lived many miles away in the jungle, but Hanuman was throwing things around, as a child will do, and something landed in the saint's hermitage. So he cursed Hanuman that he would not remember his strength unless he was reminded."

We sing the *Chalisa* to remind Hanuman of who he is, and in the very last verse, we ask him to come live in our hearts. Hanuman is the "knower of all hearts" and lives only to serve God within us and prepare us to live fully in the spirit. His entrance into our lives brings about the

fulfillment of every desire. It's not necessary to ask Hanuman for anything, for he knows all. But as human beings, we honor and express the longing of our hearts, recognizing our predicament—that we are stuck in the feeling of separateness. This reaching out destroys the sense of distance from the Beloved.

Many people fantasize about going off to a cave somewhere, far away from "the world," where they imagine they will find peace of mind and live in some state of bliss. But the truth is that the cause of our unhappiness lies within our own hearts, so no matter where we go, we take it with us. That's the bad news, but it's also the good news. If it is true, it means

सकल अमंगल मूल निकंदन

that everything we see in the supposed outer world is really a reflection of—or a reaction to—our own state of being. If we look around and see anger, fear, and suffering of all kinds, it is the result of the *way* we see, not *what* we see. Of course, horrible conditions exist, but being stuck on a superficial level, we can't see what underlies them: the vast presence in which all things have their existence. It is because of this incomplete way of seeing that each of us suffers in our own personal way.

Someone once asked Baba Nityananda if he felt pain. He said, "Yes, but not the way that you do." The great saints feel all the suffering in the world, but as Sharon Salzberg says, their hearts are "as wide as the world," wide enough to hold suffering and transform it into compassion and love for all beings. This is where all of us are headed. But how do we get there?

The way we live these days doesn't allow much time or space for spiritual practice. We are always rushing around, busy with work, family responsibilities, and our own fascination with the "stuff" of this world. We are floating down the stream of life without a way to get to the shore. Our own habits and desires conspire with our negative emotional attachments to keep us locked out of our own hearts. Even if we have the desire to do some kind of spiritual practice, the *vasanas*, or tendencies of our minds, keep us spinning around, preventing us from finding any peace.

In a bhajan, Bhimsen Joshi sings:

> *Oh Lord, I have done pilgrimage to all the*
> *   holy places,*
> *But when I do puja, all I see is my desires.*
> *How will I ever cross this ocean of life?*
> *I wash Krishna's feet in my heart,*
> *But I don't listen to what anyone tells me.*
> *Let me always stay at your feet.*

Where and how can we take refuge at those feet? The *Hanuman Chalisa* is chanted specifically to clean the mirror of our hearts so we can come into direct contact with the grace of Hanuman. His river of grace flows into our nearly dried-up stream and fills it with the water of life, awakening us to the awareness of Ram's (God's) presence within. This is when our hearts truly come alive. Once the waters of two rivers mingle, they can never be separated.

Taking refuge is a subtle and important concept. When we sincerely take refuge in a "higher power," it is an implicit recognition that we need help. More than that, it is the recognition that help *is* available. This is the beginning of developing real faith—not blind faith, but faith based on our own experience. It is opening to the realization that things are not the way we think they are, and that someone is there to help us—someone who knows what is to be known.

> Hanuman is that Mahadeva (the Great Lord),
>   Mahakala (the Cosmic Nature of Time),
> The eternal goodness,
>   The blissful one who bestows liberation,
> Allowing seekers to merge with him and attain his state,
> As well as bestowing the enjoyment of all one's cherished
>   objects of desire.

The *Chalisa* invites Hanuman to come, but we are not always ready for him. We don't believe it could happen—that so much love could come to live in us. Hanuman brings with him all the beautiful qualities of strength and gentleness, courage and fearlessness, love and compassion. More than that, he throws out all our old moldy furniture: all the unwashed pots and pans, all the old dirty clothes piled up in the corner, all our stuff, our selfish little secrets, and all we hide from ourselves and others—all the mold and dirt we have gotten used to living with! He doesn't give us time to clean up for him—he does the housecleaning himself, going from room to room throwing stuff out the windows, as we follow him around and say, "Oh no, not that too!"

Once Hanuman has moved in, then we are truly ready to begin the practice of repeating the Divine Name: Ram. The Name is a mystery. It is said that God and His Name are not different. This is not the simple mechanical repetition of sounds, but a deep and ancient path to Realization. It is the transmission of awareness of the presence of God within us.

Rajida Pande wrote in *Divine Reality:*

> *Maharaj-ji was continuously uttering "Ram, Ram . . ." Even while talking, he could be seen moving his thumb continuously around his finger as if repeating a mantra. At times he became so engrossed that he appeared to be lost in himself. He often said, "Ram's form left this world, Krishna's form left this world, but the Name stays. By reciting His Name everything is achieved," and shaking his head, he reiterated, "Everything is achieved."*

Someone once asked Maharaj-ji, "Isn't it hypocritical to worship God when you are not sincere in your devotion?" Baba [Maharaj-ji was referred to as Baba or Baba-ji, as well] *answered, "If you can't do it with true feeling and you don't want to otherwise, what will you do then? Something is better than nothing. To begin with, one may not be entirely sincere, but in due course of time, the thoughts get purified and the honesty of intention comes by itself. Can anyone have the vision of God with naked eyes? One must have divine sight to visualize him, and a person only gets it after the purification of thoughts. For this, a pious life, bhajan, and spiritual practice are essential. Go on reciting Ram, and one day the true call for Ram will come out and you will be redeemed." According to Baba, one true recitation of the Name of Ram from the heart was equal to countless recitations otherwise.*[3]

Saints from almost every tradition talk about the power of the Name. Shirdi Sai Baba said:

Saints testify that in this Name resides the power of the presence of God . . . Beginning with simple repetition, gradually but inevitably, the Divine Power, which is hidden in it, is disclosed and takes on the character of a ceaseless uplifting of the heart, which persists through the distractions of the surface life.

Ramana Maharshi said:

When singing the Divine Name becomes continuous, all other thoughts cease and one is in one's real nature, which is invocation or absorption. We turn our minds outwards to things of the world and are therefore not aware that our real nature is always invocation.

Sri Ramakrishna said:

Each and every revealed Name of the One Reality possesses irresistibly sanctifying power. Even if the energy of the Divine Name does not produce immediate results, its repetition will eventually be fruitful—like a seed fallen on the roof of a deserted house which crumbles over decades, finally enabling the germinated seed to take root. The conventional world and the conventional self are this disintegrating old structure.

Maharaj-ji often talked to his devotees about the Name:

Kishan Lal Sah often visited Kainchi to have Maharaj-ji's darshan. His devotion was such that he looked upon Maharaj-ji as God. In spite of his faith, he was experiencing some depression. It happens on the spiritual path that a devotee sometimes finds himself feeling separated from God. He was disturbed by the evil he saw in the world and by the lack of his own spiritual progress.

As he approached Maharaj-ji and bowed, Maharaj-ji began to speak to his thoughts:

"You see others trapped by Maya (illusion). Narada and Bharata were trapped by Maya. These great sages were trapped by it, so what to say about others?"

Kishan Lal thought he should ask about Maya, but before he spoke, Baba said: "This

temple and whatever is seen by the human eye is illusion. What can you do about it? Delusion makes everything look real."

Kishan thought to himself that there must be a way to be free of Maya, so Baba said, "Attachment is only dispelled by His Grace."

Kishan thought, "How can we obtain His Grace?"

Baba-ji said, "Constant repetition of God's Name, with or without devotional feeling (bhava), even in anger or lethargy, brings out His grace in the form of blessedness (mangal) all around. There is no room for any doubt about it." [4]

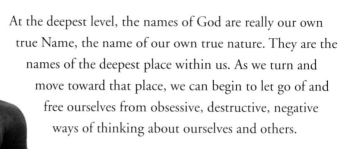

At the deepest level, the names of God are really our own true Name, the name of our own true nature. They are the names of the deepest place within us. As we turn and move toward that place, we can begin to let go of and free ourselves from obsessive, destructive, negative ways of thinking about ourselves and others.

When I was learning the *Hanumat Stavan*, another prayer to Hanuman, I came across this line: "I meditate upon Hanuman, with ruddy face and a body that glows like a mountain of gold, who can bestow all boons and fulfill all desires, and who resides under the Parijata tree, his eyes always red with tears of love for Sri Ram." It was an eye-opener for me. It means that whenever Hanuman is not busy doing special service to Ram, he is lost in love. It is through the power of his attachment to the Name of Ram, to this love, that he is freed from any attachment to the things of this world: fame and shame, loss and gain, love and hate, fear and longing.

सकल अमंगल मूल निकंदन

Hanuman is fully immersed in the Name of Ram. Wherever he is, Ram's Name will be there. Wherever Ram's Name is, there can be no room for unhappiness. It's impossible for us to imagine what this will be like. Only those who know, know. This is why we chant the *Hanuman Chalisa*. Out of our darkness we call for the light, never imagining that it will come. We keep calling with all our heart and then, finally, just when we think we can't take any more, the first rays of the dawn's light reach our hungry eyes. Amazing Grace! Hanuman's light is brighter than a million suns; his face is colored with all the beauty in this world. When he arrives, all our suffering is destroyed; we have reached the path and our way is open before us, bathed in the light of Love.

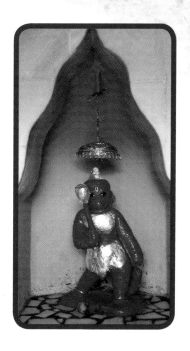

SRI NEEM KAROLI BABA

HANUMAN AND MAHARAJ-JI

 I can't write about love, compassion, strength, or wisdom—all the qualities that Hanuman embodies—without feeling the presence of my Guru, Neem Karoli Baba. Maharaj-ji was considered to be an incarnation of Hanuman. He lived for the sake of his devotees. Every minute of every day, he worked tirelessly to relieve the suffering of those who came to him. He was also constantly immersed in the remembrance of the Name of Ram.

The following are stories from some of Maharaj-ji's devotees. The first is from one of his greatest old devotees, Dada Mukerjee, from his book *By His Grace:*

> One day in the early sixties, Baba-ji came out of his room and he looked like Hanuman. I had heard from so many devotees that Baba-ji was an incarnation of Hanuman, but Didi (my wife) and I still had our doubts. The next day, Maharaj-ji asked Didi to scratch his back. She found his body to be so bulky, so big, that she was actually perspiring while trying to reach her hand across his back.
>
> In 1968, Didi did not go to Kainchi during the summer; she was in Allahabad with her mother, so I came alone. It was the day of the June 15th bhandara, the anniversary of the inauguration of the ashram. After taking his

मृगल मूरति माउत नन्दन   सकल अमृगल मूल निकृंदन

food, Maharaj-ji went around the ashram, checking on all the activity and visitors. Afterward, he went to the riverside and sat on the wall.

After that, we were walking around and Baba-ji caught hold of my hand. When he did that, I experienced such a heavy pressure that I felt my hand would break. He was leaning so heavily on me, I was afraid that if I fell down, he would also. It was early afternoon, and we came before the mandir, where many people were sitting. Baba-ji sat before the Shiva temple, my hand locked in his. He said, "Baitho, baitho. [Sit, sit.]" I wanted to extricate myself but could not.

There were a number of persons whom I knew sitting there—Brindavan Baba (the old Hariakhan Baba's successor) and many others. I was feeling as if I were suffocating, as if my breathing were coming to an end. My hand was so tight in his grip that there was no question of getting free. Then I saw not Baba-ji, but a huge monkey sitting there, long golden hair over the whole body, the face black, the tail tucked under the legs. I saw it clearly. I closed my eyes, but still I saw it. After that, I don't know what happened.

At ten o'clock that night, I found myself sitting alone down by the farm. Purnanand, from the tea shop, came and said, "Dada, here you are. We have been searching for you all evening." He took me back to the ashram.

Baba-ji had not gone inside his room yet; he was sitting on a cot and many devotees were around him. As soon as we came across the bridge and near the temple, somebody said, "Baba, Dada has come." He just said, "Accha, thik hai [very good]." There was nothing to take notice of, nothing to be excited about. I was feeling very depressed. I didn't want to talk; I just wanted to be alone and go to bed.

The next day, Gurudatt Sharma and Siddhi Didi and others kept asking me what had happened. They told me that we had been sitting there in front of the Shiva temple, surrounded by many people, when suddenly we were both missing. Then Baba and I were seen walking on the top of the hill. An hour or two later, Baba returned alone. I knew what I had seen— that it was actually Hanuman. It was not a dream, not a mistake. How the time passed, I do not have any recollection.

The next day, the normal routine started again. On the third day, I was alone with Baba-ji in his room. I said, "Now look here, Baba. I am not interested in your miracles. I have had enough. I know you are Baba and that is all I need.

This was the end of a stage in my journey. Now I had come to accept that Baba-ji was more than a human being—that he was superhuman, a divine incarnation. When I would think about him in this light, new difficulties arose. Being what he is, why did he go out of his way to show us his grace, his compassion, his help and assistance? For me, there was no question of asking him for anything, at least not for myself. I would act as the spokesperson on behalf of many of the mothers, the Westerners, and other persons, but I never asked anything for myself. Baba-ji would say, "Dada, what do you want?"

"Nothing."

"Tell me, what do you want?"

"Baba, nothing."

"Tell me. I know what is in your mind."

"So why are you asking me, then?"

He said, "Oh, I was just asking."

From the first contact I had with him in 1935, and during the second stage from 1955 when I came to know him, I resisted him. He took so much time, but never gave up or abandoned me. After having his darshan as Hanuman in 1968, whatever doubts I had were cleared away and my whole perspective changed. I was not afraid; I would speak openly and frankly to him.

One day, Mr. Barman told me, "Dada, you can talk so easily to him, but we are frightened." I said, "What is there to be frightened of? We make mistakes, we make blunders, but he is so very indulgent, so very forgiving, he doesn't mind our lapses. Doesn't he know what is in my mind, what I am going to do? If it were wrong or unworthy, he should have checked and prevented it in advance. Is it not so? Therefore, I am not frightened." [5]

Maharaj-ji inspired faith in his devotees in many ways. The following story is from Pande's *Divine Reality*:

One time, Tularam Sah, Sri Ma, Nandan Mai, Girish, and some other devotees went from Nainital to Allahabad to have Baba's darshan. Tularam would sometimes recite "The monkey took the form of a mosquito" from the Ramayana when he was with Baba. Maybe this was his way of saying that Baba was Hanuman. [In the *Ramayana*, Hanuman took the form of a mosquito to remain unseen when first entering Lanka, the city of Ravana, the demon king.]

One day, after the distribution of the morning prasad, Baba walked across his own room and went into a small adjacent room where he got his bed made on the floor. He said that he was not well, that no one should come to see him, and that he wanted to take some rest alone. He got the room closed on all sides. It was then locked on the outside, and the key was given to Tularam so that the room could not be opened by anyone else.

At noon, Sri Ma looked out the window and saw Maharaj-ji on the road outside going towards Allenganj. She immediately told the others. Tularam Sah was compelled to unlock the door to see whether Baba was in the room. He was not. Tularam Sah and Girish followed Baba and saw him climbing up the stairs of Prakash Chandra Joshi's house. Joshi-ji came out and welcomed everyone. Later, while food was being offered to Baba, the mothers and other devotees arrived from Church Lane. Baba smilingly looked at Tularam and hummed, "The monkey took the form of a mosquito." [6]

One day, Ram Dass came and sat down by Maharaj-ji's takhat (cot). He asked Baba-ji to raise his kundalini. This is a big thing. He was asking Maharaj-ji to wake him up, to free him from his attachments and illusions. Maharaj-ji said, "I don't know anything about that. Go see such and such baba, he'll do that for you."

"No, Maharaj-ji, you do it."

"I don't know anything about that. You go see that other baba, he knows all that. He'll do it for you," Maharaj-ji said.

Now Ram Dass was getting upset and demanded, "No. Maharaj-ji, you raise my kundalini."

Maharaj-ji got up off the takhat, and before going inside, he turned and looked down at Ram Dass and said, "I only know two things: Ra and Ma [the two syllables of the Name of Ram]." He went inside, leaving Ram Dass sitting there.

When Maharaj-ji said "I only know Ra and Ma," he was revealing the highest truth about Hanuman and himself. Even though Hanuman does so much service, finds Sita, kills the demons, and accomplishes all of Ram's work, *his* inner experience is of being completely immersed in Ram, with no ego sense, no sense of being the doer. This is complete and total surrender. It is because of the depth and totality of this surrender that the full power and presence of Ram can manifest through Hanuman. Through his love of Ram, seeing him in everything, experiencing his presence in all beings, he has realized the truth and lives only to serve the ultimate reality in all its forms.

THE PRACTICE

 Hanuman exists to destroy the obstacles to our realizing the same oneness he experiences with Ram. Even when difficulties happen in our lives, he never abandons us, but rather gives us the strength to live through them without our hearts being destroyed. Whatever comes to us comes as a result of our karmas. These waves of karma come from the past. How we deal with them in the present will have a great effect on what is to happen in the future and how we will be able to deal with what comes at that time. It is our own "knee-jerk" reactions—our tendencies to react out of fear or anger or selfishness to the events of our lives—that keep us spinning around.

The more we understand what is necessary to conquer these disturbing tendencies, the more we realize how difficult it will be to accomplish. It is said that Hanuman will remove the obstructions to success in any endeavor, even helping us satisfy our worldly desires. How much more will he help when we begin to turn within, toward the Beloved whom he serves, who is also longing for us.

The *Hanuman Chalisa* is chanted specifically to remove these obstacles and to destroy any negative tendencies in our hearts and minds. Maharaj-ji said, "Doing prayers like the *Hanuman Chalisa* is the only way to change fate."

The most important part of any spiritual practice is doing it. That is why we should always just "do the practice" and not be overly concerned with or focused on what we think the results might be, or even on our own state of mind. The truth is, *it can't be what we think!* It just *is!* It is not up to us to create it—we are simply cleaning the mirror of our hearts so we can see the reflection of our own true face without distortion.

God already lives within us. All we have to do is take better aim to figure out where to look. Repetition of the Name and reciting prayers like the *Hanuman Chalisa* are at once the path and the goal. They are the path when we think we are separate and we are doing it, but with deeper realization we find that Love has been waiting inside of us all along, pulling us into

सकल अमंगल मूल निकंदन

Itself. Just like a statue that slowly emerges from a slab of marble as more of the block is chipped away, we begin to experience Hanuman's inner form as our practice deepens. It already exists within. We are just removing what's covering it. As our focus and attention increase, the form comes alive within us. It is Love.

Maharaj-ji said that Hanuman is the very "breath of Ram." Ram lives and breathes in all beings as our true nature, and Hanuman is his breath, bringing life to our hearts. As we reach deeper levels of understanding and experience, the saints say that we will see as Hanuman sees—that from the beginning it was Ram himself doing everything, that what we took as *our* love and devotion was really Ram pulling us into himself. He lives in each one of us as *who we truly are.*

Once, I was talking with KC Tewari, who was not only my best friend but also my teacher. We were discussing surrender and action, and whether one should just accept and surrender to whatever comes, try to change things, or ask Maharaj-ji to do it. I was holding to the view that one should not ask anything from God but accept whatever comes. He asked me if I was happy. Of course my answer was no. He said, "So then? You are not accepting. If you could accept, you would be happy as you are. Face the fact that you can't accept, that you are not able to be at peace, and do what you can to change that and achieve happiness." I was crushed. He was right. I was totally tripping in my head about things, when the truth was that I couldn't accept things as they were, as God had given. Nor was I able to do anything about it at the time.

At some time during the 1980s, I was staying in the jungle ashram of a great saint. (He was 163 years old at the time. He's older now!) He looked at me one day and said, "You have to develop willpower." I was shocked and thought to myself, *What is he talking about? What do I need willpower for?*

Then he did something and opened me up inside, showing me exactly what he meant and what he saw in me. He showed me that I was constantly crippling myself, that I was tripping myself up at every turn and not allowing myself to jump into life. When I saw this, I couldn't believe it. Why was I doing that? No one was doing it to me; I was crippling myself. I saw that there was nothing wrong with all the things I wanted in life—the problem was that I was not allowing myself to go after and achieve them. I saw that this included so-called spiritual things. The same willpower that would propel me into the center of life would also enable me to achieve what I wanted for my inner heart. There weren't two of me, a spiritual Krishna Das and a worldly Krishna Das; it was just me in my life—and I was hardly allowing myself to live it.

Hanuman is a being who lets nothing come between him and his desire to serve Ram. He has all the energy and strength in the universe and is always serving Ram 100 percent. At that moment, I saw that I too could do this. I could live 100 percent! I just had to start mobilizing my will. It would be my will, aligned with the grace and power of Hanuman, which would bring me all I needed in life and allow me to be myself completely and to serve my Guru. This was an important moment that eventually led me to allow myself to sing *kirtan* with people.

GURU'S GRACE

If the Earth can be illumined even today by stars which disintegrated long ago, it is not impossible that the hearts of its inhabitants may be illumined, sanctified, entranced and beautified by Grace which emanates from a spiritual being vitalized long ago in the chronology of time. Like a charged battery, that spiritual entity can reveal itself, wherever there is available a receiving set attuned to it.

— *Yoga of the Bhagavad Gita* [7]

 Since the beginning of time, truth has been transmitted from Guru to disciple, from Saint to devotee, from those who know, who have realized, to those who aspire to know. Grace is always raining down on us, but we have to learn to cup our hands and catch the drops, or we will go thirsty.

I only know one thing. The love that I experienced in the presence of my Guru was far deeper and more real than any "love" I had ever felt before. It was also so much more intimate and enveloping than anything I had even dreamed of feeling or imagined that I would ever come into contact with. There is no love in me that doesn't come from him. There is no good quality in me that isn't a result of his blessings, his Grace.

One of his gifts to me, and to all of us, is the *Hanuman Chalisa*. As the great puppeteer, he is pulling all the strings from just beyond our field of vision, providing us with a way to gather the strands of all the many parts of our lives, our psyches, and twist them into a strong rope with which we can bind ourselves to the feet of True Love.

मंगल मूरति मारुत नन्दन ⑤१ सकल अमंगल मूल निकंदन

CHANTING THE
HANUMAN CHALISA

Learning to chant the *Hanuman Chalisa* takes a tremendous amount of effort and dedication. Once you are familiar with it, you can begin to use the *Chalisa* as a devotional practice. This will develop naturally over time if you are sincere about connecting to a deeper place within. Your practice will mature and change from within as your center of gravity deepens, which of course is a result of doing the practice. You can sing the *Chalisa* to a picture of Hanuman or your guru—whatever it is that helps you to connect, that enables you to make it an offering rather than a mechanical recitation. It is not necessary to understand every word, but keep in mind the general meaning of what is being sung.

I recorded the versions of the *Hanuman Chalisa* on the accompanying CDs in a simple way in order to help people learn it. The *Chalisa* does not have to be sung with a melody. It can be chanted quietly at any comfortable speed. You don't have to memorize it; you can read the words and sing along with the CDs at the same time.

I think the best way to approach learning it is to work first with the pronunciation guide on Disc 2. Once you get in the habit of mispronouncing the words, it is *very* hard to break. Take it from me! It will also help you keep a better flow when trying to fit the words into the melodies.

I jokingly refer to my pronunciation as "American Hindi." I have been singing the *Chalisa* for thirty-five years and have spent much time living in India, but I still am not a good Hindi speaker. For instance, in Hindi there are four different and distinct sounds that correspond to the letter *t* in English. But in English we just have *t,* and although it is pronounced differently in different words, we don't really notice. In India, they notice. It's the same with the letters *d, n, r,* and others.

I am not a Hindi scholar, but I have made much effort to sing this as correctly as possible—and I think I get pretty close. At least when I sing it with Indians, they know what I am singing. And Maharaj-ji liked it.

The first time we sang it to him, he stopped us and tried to correct our pronunciation of the word "*vidyawana.*" I'll never forget that. I remember getting a totally blank look on my face, as I could not for the life of me figure out what he was saying. He quickly gave up and asked us to continue. It was the last time he ever tried to correct us that way!

He honored and accepted our devotion and overlooked our pronunciation. He would often quote from the *Ramacharitamanasa,* "Ram loves only love." That being said, I think that every effort should be made to pronounce the words as correctly as possible, simply out of respect for the culture and tradition from which the *Hanuman Chalisa* springs. There is no doubt that God hears the inner calling of every heart and responds to all, but if we are going to do this as a devotional practice, the more wholeheartedly and mindfully we learn and recite the *Chalisa,* the deeper it will take us.

DISC 1: The Chants

1 Sri Ram Chalisa 16:26
2 Hallelujah Chalisa 9:42
3 Good Ole Chalisa 8:22
4 Nina Chalisa 7:32
5 Mountain Chalisa 9:54
6 Bernie's Chalisa 10:10
7 Ring Song / Jaya Siya Ram 9:38

We often add the following verse between repetitions of the *Chalisa* or between the introductory section and the body of it, as well as at the end:

maṅgala mūrati māruta nandana
sakala amaṅgala mūla nikandana

You are the embodiment of blessings, Son of the Wind.
You destroy the root of everything that is inauspicious and harmful.

Track 4 is sung by Nina Rao, my assistant. I tricked her into doing it. I told her we would sing it together, but in the studio I just sat in the group and said, "You sing." And she did, beautifully.

She also sings a couplet from the *Ramacharitamanasa*:

pavana tanaya bala pavana samānā, budhi viveka vigyāna nidhānā
kavana so kāja kathina jaga māheeṅ, jo nahin hoi tāt tumha pāheeṅ

Son of the Wind, you are as strong as the Wind himself. You are the
embodiment of intelligence, discrimination, and true wisdom. What
undertaking in this world is too difficult for you to accomplish?

The last track on Disc 1 is the original version of the "Ring Song," taught to me by two devotees of Maharaj-ji: Mrs. Tewari and her daughter, Meenu. The "Ring Song" on *Pilgrim Heart*, my second CD, came from this chant. It is Sita talking to Hanuman, who has just jumped over the ocean to find her for Ram. I thought you would enjoy it.

DISC 2: Pronunciation Guide

1　Hanuman Chalisa (slow) 7:36
2　Hanuman Chalisa (phrase by phrase) 21:28

The two tracks on Disc 2 are meant to be used over and over to learn how to say the words without having to worry about singing a melody. You'll find it useful to practice with these tracks and then go back to singing. It's harder to pronounce the words correctly when you are trying to match them with a melody and rhythm.

"a"　short "a" as in b*u*t
"ā"　long "a" as in f*a*ther
"i"　short "i" as in l*i*p
"ee" long "e" sound as in s*ee*n
"u"　as in p*u*t
"ū"　as in sch*oo*l

"é"　as in st*a*y
"ai"　as in N*a*ncy or h*e*n
"o"　as in h*o*tel
"th"　as in *t*ough, not as in *th*in
"ṅ"　nasal "n" sound like in so*ng*
"ph" as in a*pp*le not *ph*one

मंगल मूरति मारुत नन्दन　सकल अमंगल मूल निकंदन

Shree Hanumān Chāleesā
Forty Verses in Praise of Hanuman

Transliteration

shree gurū charana saroja raja nija manu mukuru sudhāri
baranoṅ raghubara bimala jasu jo dāyaku phala chāri
buddhi heena tanu jāniké sumiroṅ pavana kumāra
bala buddhi vidyā déhu mohiṅ harahu kalésa bikāra

1   jaya hanumāna gyāna guna sāgara
    jaya kapeesa tihuṅ loka ujāgara

2   rāmadūta atulita bala dhāmā
    anjani putra pawanasūta nāmā

3   mahābeera bikrama bajraṅgee
    kumati nivāra sumati ke saṅgee

4   kaṅchana barana birāja subesā
    kānana kuṅdala kuṅchita késā

5   hātha bajra o dhvajā birājai
    kāṅdhé mūṅja janéū sājai

6   shaṅkara suvana késaree nandana
    téja pratāpa mahā jaga bandana

7   vidyāvāna gunee ati chātura
    rāma kāja karibé ko ātura

8   prabhu charitra sunibé ko rasiyā
    rāma lakhana seetā mana basiyā

9 sūkshma rūpa dhari siyahiṅ dikhāvā
   bikata rūpa dhari laṅka jarāvā

10 bheema rūpa dhari asura saṅghāré
   rāmachandra ké kāja saṅvaré

11 lāya sajeevana lakhana jiyāyé
   shree raghubeera harashi ura lāyé

12 raghupati keenhee bahuta barāee
   tuma mama priya bharatahi sama bhāee

13 sahasa badana tumharo yaśa gāvaiṅ
   asa kahi shreepati kaṅtha lagāvaiṅ

14 sanakādika brahmādi muneesā
   nārada shārada sahita aheesā

15 yama kubéra digapāla jahāṅ té
   kabi kobida kahi saké kahāṅté

16 tuma upakāra sugreevahiṅ keenhā
   rāma milāya rāja pada deenhā

17 tumharo mantra vibheeshana mānā
   laṅkéshvara bhayé saba jaga jānā

18 juga sahasra jojana para bhānū
   leelyo tāhi madhura phala jānū

19 prabhu mudrikā méli mukha māheeṅ
   jaladhi lānghi gaye acharaja nāheeṅ

20 durgama kāja jagata ké jété
   sugama anugraha tumharé tété

21 rāma duāré tuma rakhavāré
   hota na āgyā binu paisāré

22 saba sukha lahai tumhāree sharanā
   tuma rakshaka kāhū ko dara nā

23 āpana téja samhāro āpai
   teenoṅ loka hāṅka téṅ kāṅpai

24 bhūta pisācha nikata nahiṅ āvai
   mahābeera jaba nāma sunāvai

25 nāsai roga haré saba peerā
   japata nirantara hanumata beerā

26 saṅkata téṅ hanumāna churāvai
   mana krama bachana dhyāna jo lāvai

27 saba para rāma tapasvee rājā
   tinaké kāja sakala tuma sājā

28 ora manoratha jo ko-i lāvai
   so-i amita jeevana phala pāvai

29 chāroṅ yuga paratāpa tumhārā
   hai parasiddha jagata ujiyārā

30 sādhu santa ké tuma rakhavāré
   asura nikandana rāma dulāré

31 ashta siddhi no nidhi ké dātā
   asa bara deenha jānakee mātā

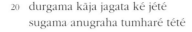

32 rāma rasāyana tūmharé pāsā
    sadā raho raghupati ké dāsā

33 tumhare bhajana rāma ko pāvai
    janama janama ké dukha bisarāvai

34 anta kāla raghubara pura jā-ee
    jahāṅ janma hari bhakta kahā-ee

35 ora devatā chitta na dhara-ee
    hanumata sé-ee sarva sukha kara-ee

36 sankata katai mitai saba peerā
    jo sumirai hanumata bala beerā

37 jai jai jai hanumāna gosā-ee
    kripā karahu gurudéva kee nā-ee

38 jo sata bāra pātha kara ko-ee
    chūtahi bandi mahā sukha ho-ee

39 jo yaha padai hanumāna chāleesā
    hoya siddhi sākhee gaureesā

40 tulasee dāsa sadā hari chérā
    keejai nātha hridaya mahaṅ dérā

    pavana tanaya saṅkata harana maṅgala mūrati rūpa
    rāma lakhana seetā sahita hridaya basahu sura bhūpa

    siyā vara rāmachandra pada jai sharanam

    maṅgala mūrati māruta nandana
    sakala amaṅgala mūla nikandana

Translation

Taking the pollen-like dust of my Guru's lotus feet
    to polish the mirror of my heart,
I can now sing the pure splendor of Sri Ram, the best of Raghus,
    which bestows the four fruits of life.

I don't know anything, so I remember you, Son of the Wind;
    grant me strength, intelligence, and wisdom,
    and remove my impurities and sorrows.

1 Hail Hanuman, ocean of wisdom;
    Hail Monkey Lord! You light up the three worlds.

2 You are Ram's messenger, the abode of immeasurable power,
    Anjani's son, named "Son of the Wind."

3 Great hero, you are a mighty thunderbolt,
    remover of evil thoughts and companion of the good.

4 Golden-hued and splendidly adorned
    with heavy earrings and curly locks:

5 In your hands shine mace and a banner;
    a sacred thread adorns your shoulder.

6 You are an incarnation of Shiva and Kesari's son.
    Your glory is revered throughout the world.

7 You are the wisest of the wise, virtuous and very clever,
    ever eager to do Ram's work.

8 You delight in hearing of the Lord's deeds;
    Ram, Lakshman, and Sita dwell in your heart.

9   Assuming a tiny form, you appeared to Sita;
in an awesome form, you burned Lanka.

10   Taking a dreadful form, you slaughtered the demons,
completing Lord Ram's work.

11   Bringing the magic herb, you revived Lakshman;
Sri Ram embraced you with delight.

12   The Lord of the Raghus praised you greatly:
"You are as dear to me as my brother Bharat!"

13   "Thousands of mouths will sing your fame!"
So saying, Lakshmi's Lord drew you to Himself.

14   Sanak and the sages, Brahma and the munis,
Narada, Saraswati, and the King of serpents,

15   Yama, Kubera, the guardians of the four quarters,
poets and scholars—none can express your glory.

16   You did great service for Sugriva;
bringing him to Ram, you gave him kingship.

17   Vibhishana heeded your counsel;
he became the Lord of Lanka, as the whole world knows.

18   Though the sun is millions of miles away,
you swallowed it, thinking it to be a sweet fruit.

19   Holding the Lord's ring in your mouth,
it's no surprise that you leapt over the ocean.

20   Every difficult task in this world
becomes easy by your grace.

21 You are the guardian at Ram's door;
   no one enters without your permission.

22 Those who take refuge in you find all happiness;
   those who you protect know no fear.

23 You alone can withstand your own splendor;
   the three worlds tremble at your roar.

24 Ghosts and goblins cannot come near,
   Great Hero, when your name is uttered.

25 All disease and pain is eradicated
   by constantly repeating your name, brave Hanuman.

26 Hanuman, you release from affliction all those
   who remember you in thought, word, and deed.

27 Ram, the ascetic king, reigns over all,
   but you carry out all His work.

28 One who comes to you with any yearning
   obtains the abundance of the four fruits of life.

29 Your splendor fills the four ages;
   your glory is renowned throughout the world.

30 You are the guardian of saints and sages,
   the destroyer of demons, and the darling of Ram.

31 You grant the eight powers and nine treasures
   by the boon you received from Mother Janaki.

32 You hold the elixir of Ram's name
    and remain eternally His servant.

33 Singing your praise, one finds Ram
    and the sorrows of countless lives are destroyed.

34 At death one goes to Ram's own abode,
    born there as God's devotee.

35 Why worship any other deities?
    From Hanuman you'll get all happiness.

36 All affliction ceases and all pain is removed
    for those who remember the mighty hero, Hanuman.

37 Victory, Victory, Victory, Lord Hanuman;
    bestow your grace on me, as my Guru!

38 Whoever recites this a hundred times
    is released from bondage and gains bliss.

39 One who reads this *Hanuman Chalisa*
    gains success, as Gauri's Lord (Shiva) is witness.

40 Says Tulsi Das, who always remains Hari's servant,
    "Lord, make your home in my heart."

    Son of the Wind, destroyer of sorrow, embodiment of
    blessings, with Ram, Lakshman, and Sita, *live in my heart*,
    King of Gods!

    Son of the Wind, embodiment of all blessings, you destroy
    the root of all that is harmful and inauspicious.

FURTHER READING

If you are interested in reading more about Neem Karoli Baba, there are four books available about him at nkbashram.org: *Miracle of Love* by Ram Dass (Hanuman Foundation); *By His Grace* by Dada Mukerjee (Hanuman Foundation); *The Near and the Dear* by Dada Mukerjee (Hanuman Foundation); *Divine Reality* by Ravi Prakash Pande "Rajida" (Sri Kainchi Hanuman Mandir and Ashram).

NOTES

1. Buddha Amitahba, *The Tibetan Book of the Dead*, ed. W.Y. Evans-Wentz (London and New York: Oxford University Press, 2000) 96, quoted in Sri Krishna Prem, *Yoga of the Bhagavad Gita* (London: Watkins, 1939).

2. Shantnovihari Dvivedi, *Bhaktraj Hanuman,* ed. Hanuman Prasad Poddar (Gorakpur, India: Gita Press, 1963) 6.

3. Ravi Prakash Pande "Rajida," *Divine Reality: Sri Baba Neeb Karori ji Maharaj* (Kainchi, India: Sri Kainchi Hanuman Mandir and Ashram, 2005) 21.

4. Pande, 45–46.

5. Dada Mukerjee, *By His Grace: A Devotee's Story* (Santa Fe, New Mexico: Hanuman Foundation, 1990) 83–85.

6. Pande, 104–105.

7. Buddha Amitahba, *The Tibetan Book of the Dead*, ed. W.Y. Evans-Wentz (London and New York: Oxford University Press, 2000) 96, quoted in Sri Krishna Prem, *Yoga of the Bhagavad Gita* (London: Watkins, 1939).

MUSIC CREDITS

Krishna Das - vocals, harmonium, finger cymbals, producer

Arjun Alan Bruggeman - tabla

John McDowell - African drums, percussion, piano, keyboards

David Nichtern - guitar, electric guitar

Genevieve Walker - violin

Nina Rao - finger cymbals, vocals, harmonium (track 4)

Kirtan response by the Ever-Changing Kosmic Kirtan Posse

Jay Messina - engineer, co-producer

Recorded at Skyline Recording Studios in New York City, May 2006

All songs published by Mustamullah Music (BMI) 2007

More information at krishnadas.com

ABOUT THE ARTIST

Krishna Das is an internationally acclaimed recording artist and cofounder of the Triloka world-music label.

His albums include *All One* (Karuna, 2005), *Greatest Hits of the Kali Yuga* (Karuna, 2004), *A Drop of the Ocean* (Karuna, 2003), *Door of Faith* (Karuna, 2003), *Breath of the Heart* (Karuna, 2001), *Live on Earth (For a Limited Time Only)* (Triloka, 2000), *Pilgrim Heart* (Triloka, 1998), and *One Track Heart* (Triloka, 1996).

A devotee of renowned Indian guru Neem Karoli Baba (Maharaj-ji), he leads chanting as a spiritual practice on the path of devotion. He tours extensively and chants with people all over the world. More information can be found at krishnadas.com.

ABOUT SOUNDS TRUE

Sounds True was founded in 1985 with a clear vision: to disseminate spiritual wisdom. Located in Boulder, Colorado, Sounds True publishes teaching programs that are designed to educate, uplift, and inspire. We work with many of the leading spiritual teachers, thinkers, healers, and visionary artists of our time.

To receive a free catalog of tools and teachings for personal and spiritual transformation, please visit www.soundstrue.com, call toll-free 800-333-9185, or write to us at the address below.

SOUNDS TRUE

PO BOX 8010 / BOULDER, CO 80306

मंगल मूरति मारुत नन्दन   सकल अमंगल मूल निकंदन